Rodin's Hands & Those of Others

Rodin's Hands & Those of Others

Poems by

Peter Prizel

© 2025 Peter Prizel. All rights reserved.
This material may not be reproduced in any form, published,
reprinted, recorded, performed, broadcast,
rewritten or redistributed without
the explicit permission of Peter Prizel.
All such actions are strictly prohibited by law.

Cover design by Shay Culligan
Cover image "Two Hands" by Auguste Rodin
in the public domain
Author photo by Peter Prizel

ISBN: 978-1-63980-795-6
Library of Congress Control Number: 2026931720

Kelsay Books
502 South 1040 East, A-119
American Fork, Utah 84003
Kelsaybooks.com

*For Charlie Prizel-Payano
& Dorothy Rising*

Contents

THE HAND	11
THE CLENCHED HAND	12
THE CATHEDRAL	13
TWO HANDS	14
BLESSING LEFT HAND	16
THE SECRET	17
THE HAND OF GOD (Holding Adam & Eve)	18
HAND OF THE DEVIL (Holding a Woman)	19
LECTURE TO THE HAND OF A SHADE	21
SMALL HAND OF ST. JOHN THE BAPTIST & THREE HANDS IN A BOX	22
THE DESPAIRING YOUTH WITHOUT LEFT HAND	23
EVE (Crossed Arms)	24
CLENCHED HAND EMERGING FROM THE FOLDS OF A BLANKET	25
AUGUSTE RODIN'S DRAWER OF LIMBS	26
THE SILENCE	27
THE FAREWELL	28
CAST HAND OF CHOPIN	29
LARGE CLENCHED HAND AND IMPLORING FIGURE	30
THE THINKER	31
THE DEFENSE OR CALL TO ARMS	32
THE AGE OF MATURITY OR DESTINY & THE PATH OF LIFE OR FATALITY	33
THE SERF	34
JEAN DE FIENNES	35
THE KISS	36
THE WAVE OF THE BATHERS	37
UGOLINO AND HIS CHILDREN	39
I AM BEAUTIFUL	41
MEDITATION	45
FALLEN CARYATID CARRYING HER STONE	46

POLYPHEMUS	48
THE FALLING MAN	49
FUGIT AMORE	51

THE HAND

Warm and cold, kind and violent.
Acrobatic, yet stiff, they make us
whole.
Tools of virtue, tools of sin,
hands are granted burdens
we take for granted.

The bronze was liquid for a moment,
when it filled the cast.
Now, it cools—hardens.
The bust of the hand freezes.
Knuckles bent,
fingers outstretched, palm up.

It leaves those in the gallery to wonder,
what thoughts went through the artist's
mind, what affliction did he want to unload
when he made this hand?

THE CLENCHED HAND

Contorted knuckles pray over the tortured palm
like Nagas over the great Vishnu.

The lines of love, of fortune, and of fame
run down the palm's center.

The River Ganges flowing
into the delta of fate.

Resistance is meaningless,
but human.

The bronze cast a testament
to alloys of our imperfections.

THE CATHEDRAL

Interspersed fingers holding up the steeple.
Are you tired? What deeds were done by you?
Your mute manual labors on display
for all to see.
When the rain comes and rinses you,
I'll still be here wondering.
What deeds were done by you?

TWO HANDS

Hand I

I reach for the sky in supplication, looking for direction.
My thumb against my index finger, my pinky
following my ring's lead, bent in a half bow
next to my middle. My palm cupped waiting to receive
you.

Hand II

Behind your wrist, my thumb against yours,
Listen to me! Come back down! I'll catch you!
I'll break your sprain. I'll caress your broken nerves.
This cold metal pedestal freezes us, but not my
concern.

BLESSING LEFT HAND

Feeble, flabby wrist,
sustaining a bent pointer.
Do you feel supported?
A cast, cast into
a foreign role
frozen in time.
Thinking of a benediction,
from now until infinitum.

THE SECRET

Bent bronze digits giving a miserly rub.
Fused from a single wrist
surrendering autonomy to greed.
The faceless sculpture too embarrassed
to show itself as human.
We all share the same sentiment at times.

THE HAND OF GOD
(Holding Adam & Eve)

God created warmth, and left his fingerprints on us.
        He put us in a kiln.
On Saturday, he sat   back,
contemplating his palette of glazes,
forgetting   that he neglected,
        an air bubble.

We EXPLODE, and so does he.
He's left to tend to the Tree of Life,
a bonsai that we continue
to trim when we
do not accept
his will.

HAND OF THE DEVIL
(Holding a Woman)

A woman suspended in an arcane era,
moaning in the clutches of evil,
trying to birth justice.

She's dilated, ready to push
humanity's thinking
into modernity.

Don't squeeze, Satan!
Don't stonewall love
in that iconic bar.

How many hands have clapped
stranger's shoulders in sympathy
over a beer?

If only I could get you
drunk so you'd let go
of this poor soul.

A woman suspended in an arcane era,
moaning in the clutches of evil,
trying to birth justice.

She's dilated, ready to push
humanity's thinking
into modernity.

LECTURE TO THE HAND OF A SHADE

A model of Adam's hand from The Gates of Hell

You always lived in Plato's Cave.
Your back facing the wall, your palm
facing the fire.

In the Garden of Eden,
you lived
in ignorance, a shadowless Peter Pan.

Now you are a Lost Boy in Hell,
blamed by younger generations—
I have compassion.

Turn around so I can wave
at you.

SMALL HAND OF ST. JOHN THE BAPTIST & THREE HANDS IN A BOX

A trinity of hands around your gaping mouth,
running counterclockwise.
Pilate's hand plucks locusts from your hair—the plague.
Herod's hand approaches your mouth to silence you.
Christ's grabs your ears, tells your soul to listen
to what you preached in life.
Three silent gestures that make you scream.

THE DESPAIRING YOUTH WITHOUT LEFT HAND

Your ribs, those flying buttresses that shelter
your heart cannot hide your pain.

Your muscles ripple over them. Carrying the air
from your diaphragm as you scream.

Behind your right arm, your cathedral's spire,
you try to conceal your disfigurement.

A lacking lone limb betraying
a beauty standard.

EVE
(Crossed Arms)

Why are you hiding your breasts?
I don't blame you
for original sin.
But I do—
for shame!

CLENCHED HAND EMERGING FROM THE FOLDS OF A BLANKET

Sculpted by Eugenè Druet

I can see the pain.
I don't need to remove the
sheet. You had the decency
to cover yourself. So, when
I found you, I had a chance
to catch my breath.

I couldn't see the pain.
I needed to look closer.
The thin, fraying veil,
with tattered ends,
you wouldn't
remove it. So,
when I tried to take
it off, I couldn't stop you
from taking your last
breath.

AUGUSTE RODIN'S DRAWER OF LIMBS

From the perspective of an amputee

Bronze, plaster, and clay.
Open palms, bent arms, curled fingers.
I'll take any one!

Never was there a silent partner
who, when lacked,
commanded so much judgment.

I've already been through
the first act of
The Phantom of the Opera.

People stared at me and gawked.
Love interests turned away, as did
perspective employers.

Still, my stump tingles,
mocking my loss.
Make me whole!

THE SILENCE

From Auguste Préault

One finger over two lips,
under sullen eyes.
Enigma's portrait.

THE FAREWELL

Arms at forty-five degrees,
wrists bent. Fingers against
lips. Eyes half-closed.
Now I just need
a setting, and a
recipient of the
kiss.

Clichés, they dull the mind
but not the heart.

CAST HAND OF CHOPIN

A study's candle follows
the fingers across the
piano. Black and white
                            keys,
                                                        sharps and flats.

They're played by a big Polish
hand in a small Parisian flat.
Wells of sound spring
from the ivory desert.
A nocturne for the caravan
of life, the wick of the study
candle.

LARGE CLENCHED HAND
AND IMPLORING FIGURE

Don't push me!
                      Let me gaze at your soft, fleshy palm
                      Let me read its library of mysteries.
                      The chapter of your life, that drives
                      you to this place.
                      Let me into your pain before your
                      abuse is bronzed for posterity.
                                             Don't
push me!

THE THINKER

A heavy heart, and a heavy head.
Reason broke free from its leash,
Passion from its muzzle.
All good intent has been lost
to a too-common union.

A crooked elbow rests on
a knee supporting a hand,
under a chin.
When the hand and arm
fall asleep, the head
will droop. Its façade
of penance over,
it will have to face
its past.

THE DEFENSE
OR CALL TO ARMS

War cannot be waged without arms.
War cannot be waged without hands.
They do not feel like our hearts.

So, we continue to summon them.
Accomplices to bloodshed,
they do as they are told.

The dying soldier supports
his weight on his sword.
The winged spirit spreads her arms.

She clenches her fists.
Both heeded the call.
The hands, they asked no questions.

THE AGE OF MATURITY OR DESTINY
& THE PATH OF LIFE OR FATALITY

Arm around my aging mistress's waist.
Arm reaching back for my lover's hand,
a shameful triptych.

When the flesh of a woman rises,
when it is leavened, I move on.
All my life, I've communed with sin.

Only now, I realize that the one hanging
on this cross of shame is my wife who
mourns the fidelity I've rejected.

THE SERF

A Handless Sculpture by Henri Matisse

My burdens were your biddings
when I had hands.

I chopped wood, felled wheat, and slaughtered hogs.
Now, I can do no more.

You cast me off,
as I can no longer

serve you or myself—
a bitter taste of freedom.

JEAN DE FIENNES

Part of the monument to "The Burghers of Calais"

Your fingers dig into your scalp,
a mine of resignation.
>The carts dredging
>up your past.

Your conscience holds the lantern
of introspection. It sifts through
>the coal of actions
>waiting to be bound.

On the altar of atonement,
flecks of gold fall from
>your nails. Making you
>look presentable for your maker.

THE KISS

The lines of adoration have
no vanishing
point.
Lust-
ful kisses may cease.
But love's embrace
is timeless.

THE WAVE OF THE BATHERS

Sculpted by Camille Claudel

Three women dancing
in a circle, under
Neptune's watery hand—
brought up by a lustful tide,
under a night sky.

Diana has made
herself scarce.
She wants her uncle to
cease the hunt. She's hid
the moon behind the clouds.

She tries to lead primal instinct
away, tries to dim the ocean's
eyes, tries to call off the hounds.

He won't stop until he sees
the bathers are here.
And when he does,
the moon will shine full.
It will make the wave
disappear into the depths,
of shame.

UGOLINO AND HIS CHILDREN

Your hands are there to break your fall!
Don't be the baby in the Sphynx's riddle
and crawl on all fours.

Don't fall, don't fall from dignity.
Get up! Help your son whom you have pushed
to the ground.

The gnawing hunger of your stomach
is nothing to that you will feel after death.
Your hands are there to break your fall!

From

Grace.

PS:
The wheat you seek to eat mourns. Its chaffs bow in sorrow in the cool summer breeze. The crickets hum a dirge in the thicket just beyond—
the moat. The nightingale waits to sing your eulogy.

I AM BEAUTIFUL

He holds me up with his hands—panting.
Frequencies of desire wash over
my nautilus-shaped ear, grant access.
None of the chamber's emissaries of love
are courted.
No tokens of affection are left, no flowers,
no kind words. His hands and mouth are too busy
for play.

RODIN'S OVERSIGHT

In your life, the gypsum on the banks of the Siene,
the plaster of Paris never fully set.
Hell never made it to the foundry in your lifetime.
Your hands never ceased shaping, never stopped shifting
morality. You were always shuffling candidates
for your monumental *Inferno*. Perhaps you felt empathy.

Did your will say to cast "The Gates"?
Did you stipulate a permanent binding
of humanity's fracture from The Almighty?
If only you had lived and kept the plaster wet.

TORSO OF ADELE

Your arms and legs an almost equilateral
triangle hanging on the tympanum.
They support your sultry breasts on the jamb of the door.

When I push it open the hinge of fornication
creaks. Fecundity, its brother below, stubbornly
does not give way.

Perhaps if I stick my arm up, rest my hand against
the frame, and complete the jamb and the tension
of sides, the door will open.

I raise my arm and guide it to the gap. I stop
midway. I gaze at your breasts, and turn
my hand toward them ready to touch them.

I then realize—Hell is all contexts.
I don't have to go through the door
to get there.

Unchecked lust without love is enough.
Again, I move my arm. I place it against
the frame. I finish the trinity of sides you started.

I hold your hand tenderly, and you squeeze
mine. We understand each other. Let someone
else venture into the darkness.

MEDITATION

I am not listening
to the screams, to the crying,
to the whimpering, and the sighing.

Against my ear is my hand;
it grabs the grief, it traps the sorrow,
it lassos the pain.

I am left to wonder if I have found mercy.

FALLEN CARYATID CARRYING HER STONE

From "The Gates of Hell" at Stanford University

A stone my shoulder.
With my arms crossed against my knee,
I support my head while my hands rest.

Why can't I be Atlas and hold up
the sky? Why must I undertake
the entrance to the Devil's abode?

Down below *The Thinker* contemplates
my grievance. I assume an 18th-century
idea in the twenty-first.

Looking down on the campus of
Stanford University, I see women.
I see strong, independent females walking.

They are free from the shackles of the household,
liberated from the restrictions in the workplace,
uninhibited by childbearing if they so choose.

Why can't I be Atlas and hold up the sky?
Why can't I hold that glass ceiling,
push these women to break through it?

The Thinker, at least grant me this honor.

POLYPHEMUS

Two to one.
You should have been able
to come through.
When I lost my eye to Ulysses,
you should have been able to
find him.

Perhaps your nerves delighted
in the soft sheep's wool,
made cool by a
Sicilian breeze.

My hands! Why did you fail me
when my eye gave way? You
let the Greeks escape.
Now you must reap callouses,
as I tear this island apart
looking for a salve
under Elba's shadow.

THE FALLING MAN

From "The Gates of Hell" at Ueno Park, Tokyo

Only as I hang over the darkness
do I realize your power.
When I killed the man in the brawl
last night, you betrayed me.

You never wanted to be in on this.
You shook as the cherry blossoms fell,
in the spring winds. Pink tears
around the corpse.

You left your marks—
your arches, loops, and your whorls.
Three fates for the police
to find and match.

They picked me up
by the man I had killed.
I was on my knees, holding
the same knife.

My shirt was up—I was ready.
The blossoms were still falling.
The full moon was watching.
All was set for my demise.

Now I am hanging over
the darkness, hearing the
cries of the man I killed.
You won't let go.

The blossoms still fall.
The moon still shines.
Pink tears, and a witness
who will never leave.

FUGIT AMORE

I simply gave in to you.
Now I wring my hands
around my head.
Your hands cup my breasts.

A bra for hell as I carry you
on my back. So those I meet
will not see what first attached you
to me. I'm an ass trapped in flight.

About the Author

Peter Prizel is an end-of-life care social worker. He has published *Fables Obscura,* a short story collection; *Verses of the Soviet Rail,* a full-length poetry collection; and two novels: *An Angelic Folly* and *The Fermented Savior.* He holds an MFA from Manhattanville College. Peter lives in the NYC Metropolitan Area with his wife and three daughters.

www.ingramcontent.com/pod-product-compliance
Lightning Source LLC
Chambersburg PA
CBHW071013160426
43193CB00012B/2039